The Eden Valley, Westmorland

IN OLD PHOTOGRAPHS

The Eden Valley, Westmorland

IN OLD PHOTOGRAPHS

Collected by JOHN MARSH

Alan Sutton Publishing Limited
Phoenix Mill · Far Thrupp
Stroud · Gloucestershire

ALAN SUTTON

First published 1992

This book is dedicated to
Betty Wainwright
A sunny Easter Sunday, 1992,
Crosby Ravensworth

**British Library Cataloguing
in Publication Data**

Marsh, John
The Eden Valley, Westmorland in Old
Photographs
I. Title
942.786

ISBN 7509–0111–X

Typeset in 9/10 Sabon.
Typesetting and origination by
Alan Sutton Publishing Limited.
Printed and bound by
WBC, Bridgend, Mid Glam.

Contents

Kirkby Stephen market place around 1905.

Introduction

This book completes a trilogy illustrating the rural areas of the old County of Westmorland. *South Westmorland Villages* (1991) covered the area south of Kendal; *The Westmorland Lakes* (1992) depicts the area north of Kendal and the Lake District parts of the county towards its western boundaries with Lancashire and Cumberland. The coverage in this volume overlaps that of *The Westmorland Lakes* on the fringes of the Shap fells and at the Ullswater to Eamont Bridge boundary with Cumberland. The great north road over the Shap fells and the northern tip of Ullswater belong to both books and must, I feel, be so illustrated.

The history of the land surrounding the Eden Valley is as ancient as any in Britain. The fell lands contain traces of the earliest human occupation which persisted until the start of 'history', the occupiers being the tribes that were absorbed by the Romans. The area of Crosby Ravensworth and the valley of the Lyvennet were, without doubt, the centre of an ancient kingdom or tribe. Academics are now revealing much of this unknown period. After the Roman period the *civitas* of Rheged is likely to have extended from Carlisle as far as the

Lyvennet. There are traces of very early Christianity at Brougham where the settlement surrounding the Roman fort appears to have remained in use, the nearby holy site of Ninekirks possibly connecting fourth-century Christianity with that of the medieval period. The ancient routeways of the Eden and the Stainmore and Shap Fell watersheds were added to by the Romans who had, besides their main route from Caterick to Carlisle, roads to the Lune from Brough and Brougham, to Alston from Kirkby Thore, to Ambleside from Brougham, to Kendal from Tebay, and also, possibly, over the Shap fells.

The Norse left their place names and speech, and some interesting pieces of carving at such as Kirkby Stephen and Lowther churches. The Norman baronial system superimposed estates centred at Brougham, Appleby, Brough, Tebay and Lowther, and to these were added the monastic estates, the chief of which was at Hepp (now Shap) where the Premonstratensian Canons enjoyed a haven of peace in the valley of the River Lowther until the destructions of the English Reformation.

The seventeenth century was one of confusion, but the work of Anne of Pembroke (or Lady Anne Clifford) is still to be seen in the area today. In the eighteenth, first the 'Old Pretender' travelled south through Appleby to Preston, and then the last battle on English soil took place at Clifton, when 'Bonny Prince Charlie' and his army skirmished with that of 'Butcher Cumberland' in December 1745. During the nineteenth century the area was transformed by the railways that opened up the district as it had never been before. The main north-west route passed through Tebay, Shap and Clifton. The Midland Railway pushed the famous 'Settle–Carlisle' line through Mallerstang and Appleby, and north-west industry's requirement of north-east coal put an east–west route over Stainmore to Penrith and Tebay.

The language of the district has been, until very recent times, the dialect based in the most part on old Norse. It is the Westmorland dialect with subtle variations due to contact with the north-east in such places as Kirkby Stephen. 'T'owd yow lowped ower t'yat to ga wi't gut hog in't intak' would be understood all over Westmorland, and possibly in Scandinavia too. The modern name of Shap is, without doubt, the result of some off-comer recording the name after making enquiry of a local. 'S'Hepp', meaning 'It's Hepp', was understood as 'It's Shap'. Scribes and map makers have renamed many places by the same process. Modern pressures on language through radio and TV, as well as social affectations, are not leaving much of the old language for future generations, although throughout the period covered by these books the use of dialect was commonplace in most parts of society.

Our century is notable also for the siting of a huge tank/gun range on part of the Warcop fells, extensive quarrying at Shap, Kirkby Thore and Kirkby Stephen, the intrusion of the M6, the sale of Appleby Castle by the successors of the families who had occupied it for many centuries, and the demolition of Lowther Castle and Brougham Hall. This book catches the area before these modern events had taken place, a rural area of villages occupied by families who had lived there for centuries, when the main mode of transport was the railway and the horse. Odd photographs from the post-war period illustrate something now no more. The horrors of the old A6 motor road over Shap had yet to start when most of the illustrations were taken.

Where possible the name of the photographer is given with the picture. Many are local photographers who used their craft to make a living publishing post-card views of scenes or buildings. Some pictures are by national companies who traded throughout the land, visiting even remote areas looking for subjects and outlets. Odd corners of the area cannot be found in this book as photographs of them are difficult to find; I apologize to people who happen to live in these hamlets.

The famous of this area were very famous indeed in their time. Michael Faraday, Lord Chancellor Brougham, Thomas Lord Wharton, the 'yellow earl' Lord Lonsdale, and Lady Anne Clifford are among those that are included. The book also touches on the lives of the many more who were not at all famous but were as much a part of the county of Westmorland in their own way.

The author spent some of the happiest years of his life with the folk of Kirkby Stephen and there observed, although it was not realized at the time, the end of an era, as the roads were 'improved' and the railways closed. Various photo-graphs I took at the time show a much changed town. There were shopping trains to Darlington or Penrith, and London, Leeds or Manchester could easily be visited by train. The town was awake all night with the coming and going of railwaymen. Brough Hill and Appleby Fairs were very much horse transport gatherings. The quarry loads went by rail, leaving Hartley a delightful rural retreat. Many houses had no TV and some were without electricity. The town had its own gasworks. The headmaster was also the Chairman of the Magistrates; Mr Parrott will be long remembered for his humanity with both children and offenders. The cinema played records by request before perfor-mances, and the local bus services stopped as near as they could to a passenger's destination. This caring community welcomed my wife and me as though we belonged. The Westmorland of those days, that started to die well before the 1974 change to Cumbria is, I hope, captured for all to remember by this and its two companion volumes.

John Marsh
Spring 1992

SECTION ONE

The Western Fringe: Shap Fell and Tebay to Clifton

Hucks Brow about 1925, by Atkinson and Pollitt of Kendal. The Huck family, who gave their name to this notoriously dangerous stretch of road on the A6 over Shap fells, had lived in the parish of Fawcett Forest for many generations and were resident at Hollowgate Farm at the time. Note the trunk telephone line system which followed the route of the Heronsyke to Eamont Bridge turnpike road, which this was part of, from Burton to Penrith.

The same view about 1905, by J. Sawyers of Kendal. Very rarely did Mr Sawyers put his name on the picture but this photograph is an exception. On the far left is the very old coach road, marked by a wall.

Scottish hunger marchers with police escort wend their way south over High Borrow Bridge on 2 February 1934. This picture was provided by Mrs Knowles (née Huck) of Hollowgate. The protest was against the Unemployment Bill and the means test introduced by the coalition government. The *Westmorland Gazette* carried a report from the Lancashire County Council meeting where the Act was described as 'a Bill for the stabilization and standardization of starvation'. The Bryan Lancaster Trust accommodated the men in the Stramongate School in Kendal overnight.

Accidents, such as this fatal one which coincided with the widening of the bridge at the foot of Hucks Brow, were once commonplace, the men from Hudsons of Milnthorpe performing nearly impossible tasks with their recovery vehicles. Before the M6 was opened, the A6 over Shap was a very dangerous road indeed. The photograph is again from the collection of Mrs Knowles who, for many years, looked after the Leyland Clock about half a mile south of this scene.

Chemical dyes were being carried on this 15-ton lorry which crashed just north of High Borrow Bridge in July 1930. Four people on the solid-tyred lorry were injured. Another picture from Mrs Knowles's collection; the last three photographs are used with the kind permission of the editor of the *Westmorland Gazette*.

The summit of Shap Fell, an unmade road and the trunk telephone line in the 1920s, by Atkinson and Pollitt of Kendal. It was the descent from here that proved to be the end of many a motor vehicle as the A6 dropped steeply down Hucks Brow to High Borrow Bridge.

Shap Fell Pink Rock Quarry is in the background of this Sweeten's of Penrith view of the A6 north of Shap Summit. It was possible to stroll on a road which was hardly wider than a single carriageway. This just post-First World War picture shows the unmade road and the trunk telephone line in the valley bottom.

Shap Fell road from the Pink Rock Quarry railway, with the quarry cottages just below. This Matthews of Bradford picture is from the early 1920s and is the reverse view to the last picture. The railway line connected the granite works and the quarries with the London and North Western Railway sidings at Shap Summit.

The snow post markers line the side of the unfenced A6 at Roman Corner between the Pink Rock Quarry and Shap Wells in this 1930s picture by Atkinson and Pollitt of Kendal. The line of the old coach road on the left of the picture is marked by the edge of the dark-coloured heather patch.

HAP WELLS HOTEL, WESTMORLAND.

The Shap Wells Hotel in 1936, when Robert James Clark was the licensee. In a few years this hotel was to become a prisoner of war camp for German officers, a prospect it is unlikely the people on the picture were contemplating.

The Hall, Shap Wells Hotel

Two views of the interior of the Shap Wells Hotel when Mr R.J. Clark and his wife Alice were the proprietors. The top view is from the 1920s, with the notice behind the ladies offering a motor car for hire. The second picture is from the early 1930s, showing the dining room set for dinner. 'The cloth with the ink stain is where we sit' says the postcard of April 1933 to Master Bindloss of Eccles, Manchester.

THE DINING ROOM,
SHAP WELLS HOTEL.

Birkbeck Force, Shap Wells in a view from about 1905, one of a series drawing attention to the attractions of the Shap fells as a holiday resort. Mrs Dinah Stubbs was the proprietor in those days.

Low Wood, Shap Wells was another view in this turn of the century series. 'Lovers Walk' was another. The hotel offered 'Board in public room' for 7s. a day, 'In private room 8 shillings and six pence. Beds included if more than two nights.'

The Pump at Shap Wells was on the well that gave the place its name. Here, to quote a guide, 'the waters are very efficacious, in several diseases'. Discovered in the eighteenth century, the well was also said to approach the quality of Leamington water. 'The mineral waters spring from a bank near the junction of the old red sandstone and the alternate slate rocks which here assume the form of a felspar porphyry and conglomerate; but . . . there is nothing to indicate . . . from which they derive their saline properties.' This 1920s picture comes from the time of Mr R.J. Clark. Locals declared that the water tasted of 'train smoke mixed with bad eggs'.

The Blue Rock Quarry, Shap about 1908. This, remarkably, was a holiday postcard sent to Carlisle in August 1909, 'but you have to be careful what you say on a postcard here' says Maggie to Miss Ellen Young. The blue rock and the pink rock granite quarries were worked by The Shap Granite and Patent Concrete Company Ltd who, in 1905, employed 250 men producing beautifully polished stone for memorials and facing work, stone building blocks, granite paving slabs, railway ballast and road stone.

The M.A. Shepherd Rae fountain of 1896 at Shap, in an Atkinson and Pollitt picture of about 1920, shows the unmade road with the Road Traffic Act 'Slow' sign which, for many decades, greeted northbound motorists on the A6 road. 'Having a ripping time,' says the holiday postcard. 'I am sure you would like this place though it is rather hilly.'

The Station Temperance Hotel, Shap about 1905. Luncheons and Teas as well as Refreshment Rooms are advertised. 'Raining in torrents', says the holiday postcard of August 1907. Besides Alexander Murray's Temperance hotel, there was one run by James Ruddick, along with his limestone quarry and building business.

The Greyhound Hotel, Shap about 1905, when William Macdonald was shown as victualler. This was originally a coaching inn where coach horses were changed and travellers fed and lodged. Rooms were 2s. a night, breakfast from 1s., lunch 2s. and tea from 1s. at the time of the photograph.

'The New School', Shap about 1914, photographed by Thompson Brothers of Kendal in their 'Avenue' series. Originally, the 'moot hall' was on this site but this was demolished in 1838. The door dating 1688 from the 'moot hall' was incorporated in the original school and then moved to the front of the 'new' school in the alteration of 1912/13.

Carl Lofts, Shap about 1910 when John Midworth, fitter, offered apartments. 'Me and the two children are at Shap on holiday for a week or so . . . this is the view of the house,' says the postcard. The Carl Lofts name is taken from the ancient avenue of stones which was at this end of Shap village.

The Parish Rooms, Shap in the 1930s, photographed by G.P. Abraham of Keswick. Said to have been built with stone taken from Shap Abbey in the seventeenth century, this building has seen many uses, of which being the Parish Rooms was only one.

Main Street, Shap in the early 1920s, by Atkinson and Pollitt of Kendal. The sheep pass Mr J. Fairer's Verdun House. Joseph Fairer returned from Asby to Shap, where the family had lived for many centuries, in 1855 to establish his drapery and tea dealing business. Four generations of the Fairer family carried on the trade until final closure in 1981.

Cricket match at Shap in 1909 – Married versus Single. 'Not Out', in his 'Cricket Notes and News' in the *Mid Cumberland and North Westmorland Herald*, records how, in 1909, the Shap village cricket team collapsed from being the local league leaders to a position of 13th out of 23 after batsman Rosterne left. He also recorded how a heifer ate a Culgaith batsman's braces at one match.

The garage at Shap in the late 1920s, by Atkinson and Pollitt of Kendal. Founded at the smithy on the opposite side of the road by Tom Simpson, with assistance from his brother Ted, the present garage site was originally developed as a cycle shop.

The Girls Friendly Society huts, just north over the railway bridge from the garage, were one of the reasons why so many holiday postcards were sent from this most unlikely of holiday resorts. Senior Guides and GFS staff are seen here in the 1920s – all girls together. Note how the main building back wall was strengthened against the west wind by timber supports.

The A6 road and the Girls Friendly Society huts in the 1920s, by Atkinson and Pollitt. This was to prove a not very peaceful place to stay as the A6 road traffic built up over the next decades.

The old road to the south from Shap Abbey is marked with stepping stones where the River Lowther crosses the route. A group are seen testing their daring. Stepping stones were a highlight on many Victorian and Edwardian holidays and these stones were one of the holiday attractions of the Shap area. Such simple pleasures are lost today as stepping stones are removed.

The bridge north of Shap Abbey, by Lilywhite of Sowerby Bridge. Sheep have, over the centuries, been the main produce of the Abbey and the farm that followed the Abbey after the Reformation.

Shap Abbey Farm about 1908. Said to have been the Abbot's lodgings at the Abbey before the Reformation, the farmhouse was occupied by Edward de Vere Irving at the time of the photograph, the family having been there since the mid-nineteenth century.

The tower of the Abbey of God and Saint Mary Magdalene at Shap in about 1910. The Premonstratensian (or White) Canons had founded their Abbey at Preston Patrick in the 1190s but moved to this very remote spot at Hepp before 1201. Many local noble families supported the Abbey, the Redmans of Levens notably having an Abbot of Shap who also became Bishop of Ely in 1501. The Canons also ran a leper hospital in Appleby. Dissolved in 1540, the Abbey and its lands were given to Sir Thomas Wharton, a friend of Henry VIII.

The Kern Waterfall near Shap was obviously considered a suitable subject for a holiday postcard. 'Shap is undoubtedly an excellent residence,' says Pearson's gossipy guide, 'and far more bracing than more famous resorts such as Patterdale or Grasmere which lie in the hollow of deep, narrow valleys. Lodgings in the village are numerous.'

The Hanging Rock at Hardendale Nab was another natural feature which the photographer hoped would sell well on a holiday postcard. Articles in the *Cumberland and Westmorland Herald* and the *Westmorland Gazette* of May 1983 testify to recent attempts to save this interesting feature against the thoughtless actions of the staff of the British Steel Quarry. Unfortunately the Hanging Rock is now no more.

Keld Bridge, near Shap in the 1920s, by Atkinson and Pollitt of Kendal. The River Lowther is now the boundary of the Lake District National Park.

The Old Chantry Chapel, Keld near Shap is the title of this postcard from about 1910. Said to have been built by the Canons of Shap Abbey, this building is now owned by the National Trust having been a house and then a storage barn.

Keld in the 1930s, by Atkinson and Pollitt. 'An ancient village near the ruined Abbey,' says a guide book. Surrounded by ancient remains from pre-Roman up to medieval times, and with a Norse name, Keld can claim to be at the heart of the history of Westmorland.

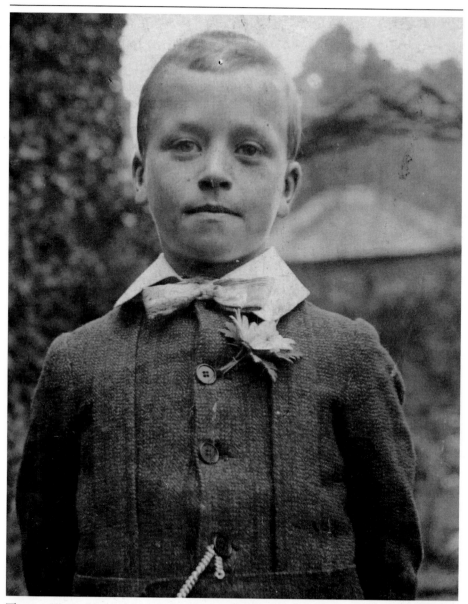

Thomas Victor Martindale, aged 9 years in 1907, got himself into the newspapers and onto a series of picture postcards when he was on holiday at John Bland's, High Howe, Bampton. Thomas had set off with Vickers Bland, the son of the farmer, to look for a pony lost on the fells. After they split up to look for the horse Thomas was not seen again, in spite of many searches, until four days later, when he was discovered near Troutbeck Park. His father walked over to Troutbeck near Ambleside to collect him and the pair then walked back to Penrith via Ullswater. His account of wandering, lost in the mists on the fells, and his survival without food caught the imagination of many at the time.

Aberdeen Express on Shap Summit is the title of this 1904 picture for the London and North Western Railway 'revised series' of November 1904. The LNWR 2–4–0 engine and nine carriages approach the summit. Shap Summit was the highest point on the LNWR's line from London to Carlisle, at 916 ft above sea level. The summit was, at the time of the picture, the scene of much activity, with 'banking' engines and Shap Granite works traffic.

Great Strickland church by A.C. Fallowfield, photographer of Penrith. The church of St Barnabas was built in 1870. The parish name means the land of the young cattle, and an interesting variation on the story of the commons enclosure here is that the tenant of a piece of land known as Bull Land must provide a bull for local farmers to use.

The Thornborrow family at Dallam Bank, Great Strickland pose at haymaking time in about 1910 with their servant lad on the extreme right. From left to right: Dick, George, Emily, Noble, father George with the rake, Clara.

Hackthorpe Hall about 1910, with Tibby Thompson at the gate. The hall is said to have been built in the early seventeenth century by Sir Christopher Lowther as a dower house for his second wife, but is now a farmhouse on the Lowther estate.

The village of Hackthorpe about 1905, by Reeds of Penrith, showing the A6 road to the south. 'A quaint village in the vicinity of Lowther castle', said the Ullswater Steam Navigation Company Guide of the time. The quaintness, like that of Shap and Clifton, was to be destroyed for over thirty years as the motorized traffic on the A6 road increased.

Clifton School about 1905, when Walter Henry George was listed as 'Schoolmaster, Assistant Overseer and Clerk to the Parish Council'. The school was built in 1876 and enlarged in 1901. Governors were Plaskett Gillbanks of Park View, Capt Edward Addison of Fair View, Joseph Hindson of Clifton Hall Farm and the Revd William McClelland Keys Wells of the Vicarage.

The Rectory at Clifton about 1905, when the vicar was William McClelland Keys Wells MA. The church next door is one of the small gems of Westmorland and dates back at least to Norman times. The last battle on English soil took place near Clifton in December 1745, troopers from both English and Scots sides having graves here.

The A6 road at Clifton with the railway bridge over the London and North Western Railway in the distance. This view was on a Christmas postcard sent to Chorley on 24 December 1909.

Bampton Old Mill and Bridge is the title of this late 1920s picture by Atkinson and Pollitt of Kendal. The mill is now no more.

Bampton, by S.M. Gibson of Gateshead in about 1908, showing just the house in the background of the previous picture. More of the Bampton area is to be found in *The Westmorland Lakes in Old Photographs*.

Morland village with farm horses in about 1918, by Friths of Reigate. A way of life with horses and carts was drawing to a close.

Main Street (or Water Street), Morland in the early 1930s, by Lilywhite of Sowerby Bridge, is a view with a motor car instead of horses. The card was posted on 1 March 1934 to Master Hutchinson of Oaktye, Crook, Kendal. 'I wonder if there is anyone on this card you know. I think there will be – Mother.'

The Morland Ploughing Association meeting of 1913, when Robert Ewin of Hall Farm, Newby was the secretary of the Association, photographed by Elliott Jordison of Penrith. Ploughing matches were popular events attracting crowds of local people.

St Lawrence's church, Morland dates back to before the Normans. This 1930s view, from the R.K. Dent of Morland series on the village, clearly shows the tower claimed to be the oldest in the county. Obviously intended for a larger town than today, a town with charters for a market and an annual fair, the church has additions from most centuries from the eleventh.

Morland, by Elliott Jordison of Penrith, about 1910, showing a policeman with his cycle and others on the unmade road. Constable Joseph William Wren was the Cumberland and Westmorland Constabulary policeman at Morland at the time.

Jackdaw Scaur at Kings Meaburn includes jackdaws painted in by the photographer Elliott Jordison. (The birds were a nuisance to the villagers as they blocked up the chimneys at nesting time.) The name of the village is said to derive from the land's being seized by the Crown after Hugh de Morville, the then landowner, assisted in the assassination of Archbishop Thomas Becket at Canterbury in 1170.

Newby (or Newby Stones) village, photographed by Nicholson and Cartner of Carlisle. The post office was 'at Mrs Barbara Ewin's'. Letters arrived at 7.55 a.m. 'via mail cart' and were despatched at 3.45 p.m. to quote a guide of the times. Robert Byers of Fernlea was Chairman of the Parish Meeting and Joseph Thompson Camplin of Newby Head was Clerk and assistant overseer.

The mill at Maulds Meaburn when Thomas Fishwick was the 'Victualler farmer and carrier to Penrith' at the Bay Horse Inn next door, with competition coming from Abraham Furness who was listed in exactly the same way at the Mason Arms. At the turn of the century William Bowman had the mill as a corn mill, but this ancient water-powered mill was also used as a saw mill at times.

Maulds Meaburn post office about 1905 when Robert Hodgson, draper and grocer, was also postmaster. 'Letters arrive via Shap 8.10 a.m., despatched 4.15 p.m. (winter 3.15 p.m.)' says a guide of the times.

Stepstones cross the Lyvennet at Maulds Meaburn about 1905, by Broughton of Burnley. The stones supplemented 'a neat bridge', to quote Bulmer's guide, 'provided in 1860 by Wilkinson Dent of Flass, costing about £552.'

Flass House, Maulds Meaburn, on a card posted 1912 saying 'this is where B.G. Cook lived.' The home of the Dent family for many years, Flass was occupied by Robert Wilkinson Dent JP, MA (Cantab) at the time of the picture.

Sleagill, by Elliott Jordison, a view used as New Year card to Miss Stephenson of Gaythorne Hall, Crosby Ravensworth about 1905. The population then was 115 people. Thomas Geldart from New Mill Flat was District Councillor and Chairman of the Parish Meeting, and Miss Annie Geldart was schoolmistress. John Bowman Wharton was at the Royal Oak.

Two views of Crosby Ravensworth from about 1905. Children can be seen on the bridge behind the Butchers Arms in the first picture. This was the ancient road from north to south until the eighteenth century; kings and armies came this way. The second photograph shows the Butchers Arms inn, commemorating 'Butcher' Cumberland who chased Prince Charles Edward's armies over the Shap fells in December 1745. The inn was run by Mrs Hannah Johnson when the picture was taken.

The view from the church tower at Crosby Ravensworth about 1905. The Revd C.J. Gordon was then the incumbent, appointed in 1901 by Lt-Col J.F. Bagot of Levens Hall near Kendal. St Lawrence's church dates from at least the twelfth century, and academics now say that the local Smythson family of masons from Crosby Bank, who may have been involved with the building of Shap Abbey tower, may also be the builders of the tower here. After the Reformation they are reported to have done work for Thomas, Lord Wharton who had acquired Shap Abbey lands from the King.

Inside Crosby Ravensworth church in the 1920s, by Atkinson and Pollitt of Kendal, with lighting by oil lamp. Major alterations in 1809–16 and 1873–6 altered the old church considerably.

The Village Hall, Crosby Ravensworth in the late 1920s when it was very new. The hall was built in 1927 as a memorial to those of the village who served in the First World War.

Orton Hall is the title of this photograph posted 23 May 1910 to Miss V.V.C. Dent at Flass, Maulds Meaburn from C.C. Crompton at Orton Hall. 'A fine old mansion built about 1662,' says a guide.

Town Head, Orton, by Rothery, printer of Orton, in about 1902 when Misses Mary Ann, Eleanor and Hannah Rothery are shown as dressmakers, drapers and shopkeepers.

Low Road, Orton, by Thompsons of Kendal in their 'Avenue' series. In those days the children could parade their dolls' prams with safety.

Church & Vicarage, Orton.

J. Simcoe & Son
Kendal

The church and vicarage at Orton about 1910. 'The Revd Doctor Burn, joint author of Nicholson and Burn's *History of Cumberland and Westmorland*, held this vicarage from 1736 until his death in 1785,' says a guide. All Saints' church is as ancient as any in Westmorland and was part of the domain of the Augustinian Canons of Conishead Priory, Ulverston (like St Leonard's at Scalthwaiterigg) until the Reformation. The heap of stones is for filling in potholes on the unmade road.

The children of Orton Council School about 1920, from Mr and Mrs F. Nevinson's collection. Orton's original school dates from 1730 but Miss Margaret Holme helped build larger premises in 1809. Miss M. Page was the mistress at the time of the photograph. A very serious occasion!

The Duke of Cumberland inn at Orton about 1905 when William Holme was listed as licensee and farmer. This inn is said to date to 1632 and had given lodging to the 'Butcher', or 'Stinking Billy' as the Scots called the Duke of Cumberland, in the eighteenth century.

The Waverley Hotel, pictured by J. Simcoe and Son of Kendal in the 1920s. This was a Temperance hotel run by Samuel Harrop Shepherd. Note the open tourer car, registration number EC3152.

Greenholme School about 1927, again from the collection of Mr and Mrs F. Nevinson. The teachers are Miss Mallinson and Mr Laing and the children are from the Bainbridge, Wilson, Hully, Longmire, Potter, Allen, Woolridge, Watson, Thwaites, Kipling, Bracken, Pratt, Dodd, Thackeray and Taylor families among others. The school dates from 1733 and was founded as a 'free school'.

Roundthwaite, Tebay in the 1930s, by Ralphael Tuck and Co. In those days the Allison, Birtle, Blamire, Brennand, Gregg, Jackson, Lowis, Mitchell, Parsley, Sergeant and Wilson families all gave Roundthwaite as their address.

The London and North Western Railway station at Tebay was a junction to Kirkby Stephen and the north-east and to the Sedbergh and Ingleton line as well as the main line station for the London to Scotland line. There were extensive sidings used for goods traffic. WH Smith had a bookstall on the station and, in 1905, J.C. Walker had the refreshments rooms while James Scott was the station master, his chief clerk being Robinson John Major. Most of the villagers worked for the railway, many being engine drivers. Cenas Thomas Brockbank was engine driver and parish clerk. Another driver had the name Garibaldi Stuart Partridge. William Askew is shown as signalman and chapel keeper.

A northbound express approaches Tebay about 1920, by J. Simcoe and Son of Kendal. Much of the land in the background was in the county of Yorkshire, and in the centre of the picture, showing as a light patch, was the site of the gallows for the medieval township of Tebay. The Roman road from Lancaster to the north crosses the picture on the Yorkshire side of the River Lune.

Woodend Terrace cottages in Tebay about 1920, by J Simcoe and Son of Kendal. 'Built by J. Wharton 1865,' says the date stone on the cottage second from the left.

Tebay School about 1920, with a field gun relic of the First World War. This picture by Atkinson and Pollitt was probably taken by Harold Simcoe, their first photographer. Tebay Endowed School dates from 1672 but was rebuilt in 1863. The Tebay Conservative Club of 1889 can also be seen.

J. Simcoe and Son's picture of Tebay church probably includes Harold Simcoe's daughter Nancy. St James's church was erected in 1880 using architect C.J. Ferguson and paid for by the London and North Western Railway and subscriptions by railway workers. The yellow with red banded brick-faced interior is a reminder of its railway origins.

The Primitive Methodist Flower Festival procession, July 1906. 'The parade assembled at Whinfell Terrace,' said the *Westmorland Gazette* of 21 July, 'and, led by the Temperance Band, moved to Old Tebay and back to a service conducted by the Revd William Batty of Dent.'

Tebay Endowed School about 1905, when the managers were Revd J.W. Hartley, vicar of Tebay, William Atkinson JP of Gaisgill, Matthew Burra JP of Raisbeck, Robert Whitehead, farmer of Ellergill, John Binks of Mount Pleasant, engine driver, church-warden and Chairman of the Conservative Association, and Thomas Wharton, farmer of Low Cock Lake, Chairman of Parish Council and County Councillor. William Ridley Stephenson was headmaster and Miss M.E. Nutter infant mistress.

The River Lune and the railway provide the background for this Atkinson and Pollitt view from the 1920s. Since 1970 the M6 motorway follows the same route towards the Crosby Ravensworth Fell.

The Tebay to Kendal road crossing the Lune near to where the M6 has now changed the scene. This is another Atkinson and Pollitt view of the 1920s.

The view from the other side of the bridge about twenty years earlier. What would the man by the fence think today? This is now on the line of the M6 motorway! This, the narrowest part of the Lune Valley and a place of harsh beauty, has been destroyed forever by the railway and the M6.

The Lune Valley above Carlingill, by Atkinson and Pollitt, about 1925. The telephone lines on both sides of the road have since gone, and the fields between the road and the Lune now carry the M6.

The unmade Kendal to Tebay road, with the Roman fort on the left and the railway bridge in front. This view, much changed today, was used by the Kodak company to advertise their 'real photographic printing by automatic machinery' on a pre-First World War advertising card.

The Tebay to Kirkby Stephen Express was the title of this picture that takes us into the area of the Lune and the Eden sources. This Valentine card was typical of a humorous style much loved in Edwardian times, and the publishing of a card for this line says much about the extent of the passenger trade on the line that connected the North Eastern Railway to the North Western Railway via Tebay junction.

SECTION TWO

The Eden

The Ulldale Waterfall at Ravenstonedale was one of those holiday places where, after a lengthy walk, a picnic could be enjoyed against a natural feature of some significance. Children and adults pose against the waterfall in about 1920. Maps, postcards and guides differ in the spelling – Uldale or Ulldale?

'Leaving Newbiggin-on-Lune' is the title given by Atkinson and Pollitt of Kendal to this view from the 1930s of what was then the main road from Kirkby Stephen to Tebay. 'The compliments of the season' from Mrs Mounsey, Newbiggin-on-Lune post office is written on the back of the card.

St Aiden's church at Newbiggin-on-Lune about 1902. This tiny church was built near the ancient holy well at Newbiggin in 1892 by John Fothergill of Brownber and was only a few years old when the picture was taken. It is reported to have cost £2,000 to build. St Helen's Holy Well, a very early Christian site, has been neglected for many centuries, and St Aiden's church is now a house.

The view across the fields to the railway station at Newbiggin-on-Lune about 1910. The railway station on the line from the north-east to Tebay was owned by the North East Railway company and, in spite of its location, was called Ravenstonedale.

A rural view from the 1930s by Atkinson and Pollitt shows the scene near Smardale Glen, Ravenstonedale. This is an ancient landscape, with many settlement sites and boundary banks on adjoining fells. The origins of the county of Westmorland are to be found hereabouts.

Ravenstonedale railway station in the late nineteenth century. 'The erection of the South Durham Railway has placed Ravenstonedale in easy communication with the world outside its own hills,' says a guide book of the time which lists William Jackson as the station master.

The Smardale Gill viaduct about 1905, showing the single track over the bridge obviously built for two tracks. The message on the back, to Master Metcalfe of Castlethwaite, Mallerstang from his sister Rachel Alice, says, 'Ask Hannah from me how the cat is coming on that got the castor oil.'

Elm Lodge and Endowed School, Ravenstonedale about 1905. The endowed school was founded in 1688 but was completely rebuilt on the same site in 1873 'at the sole cost of the late R. Gibson of Coldbeck: the upper room also serves as a Public Hall', says a guide. In the background is Elm Lodge, 'the seat and residence of T. Metcalfe-Gibson Esq'.

The Main Street, Ravenstonedale in the 1930s, by Atkinson and Pollitt of Kendal, showing a road surface 'improved' after tar spray, and a farm implement being drawn by a horse. On the left, with the small notice on the wall, is the post office then run by Thomas Wilkinson.

The Bishop of Carlisle consecrates a new portion of churchyard in this view of the church of St Oswald at Ravenstonedale. This is an ancient church site, the present church built in 1744 to replace a 'large and handsome church'. Ruins of the medieval monastic settlement on the site can now be seen in the churchyard.

Haymaking with a sledge, or sled, on Ash Fell on 18 September 1909. The use of this ancient carriage without wheels suited the steep, rough land worked by many Westmorland farmers. The tracks made by the sleds down the valley sides can be seen in most Westmorland valleys.

Joseph Dixon and his son Leonard pose with a heifer at Crooksbeck Farm, Ravenstonedale in 1904. The arrival of photography a generation or so earlier had allowed farmers to be pictured with prize beasts, pet animals and animals 'off to market'.

Fell End Angle School pupils pose for the camera in September 1906 when Miss Annie Clark, who lived at Greenslack next to the school, was the mistress. This was obviously a very serious affair, only one boy and one girl daring to wear the faintest of smiles.

Hell Gill, Mallerstang is where the River Eden starts its long journey to the sea near Carlisle. This end of the Mallerstang valley, at 1,321 ft above sea level, is the boundary with the county of Yorkshire. The bridge to be seen is Devil's Bridge. The view is by Walter Benton of Glasgow in about 1912.

IN DISASTER
GILL MOOR DEC. 24-1910.
PHOTO-HUTCHINSON.

Christmas Eve 1910 was wild and wet. Just over the boundary with Yorkshire, north of the Lunds viaduct between the Moorcock and the Aisgill summit, the St Pancras to Glasgow night express, carrying many on the way home to Scotland for Christmas on the Midland 'Settle–Carlisle' railway, ran into two pilot engines returning to Carlisle. The signal man at Hawes junction, a Mr Sutton, had sent the pilot engines on by mistake and the result was that the express, pulled by two engines and travelling at 60 m.p.h., hit the two pilot engines at about 6 a.m. Witnesses stated in the *Mid Cumberland and North Westmorland Herald* that the restaurant car took fire about half an hour after the crash which caused the carriages also to be gutted. Twelve people died, many being 'roasted alive' as they lay trapped in the wreckage. Doctors Walker and Gibson from Kirkby Stephen attended, with others from the Dales, and the *Herald* of 31 December records harrowing details such as the conversations between helpers and those being burned alive, and the description by father James Gray of his trapped infant daughter Nellie being engulfed by the flames. It is doubtful if a newspaper today would carry such a detailed report. Photograph by Hutchinson.

Outhgill at the turn of the century. From this remote hamlet, the village smith James Faraday took his wife and two children off to London where a third child Michael was born in 1791. He became a scientist famed all over the world for his experiments with electricity.

Mallerstang chapel of St Mary at Outhgill is said to date back to the thirteenth century. It was extensively restored by Lady Anne Clifford in 1663. The photograph is from the time of the Revd William Alnwick who was the vicar from 1878 to 1907.

'Old Cooper', who lived at Bollam Gate, Kirkby Stephen, was the postman who covered the Mallerstang valley at the turn of the century. He walked to Thrang and back six days a week and on three days went on to Aisgill moor. As an ex-militia man at the time of the Boer War he gained a reputation for his views, freely given, on war and peace.

The Thrang was where Postman Cooper ended his round on many days. This photograph of about 1910 shows the 1833 house built by the Revd John Fawcett with the extension of 1908 by the Revd E. Simpson. The chimneys show the signs of the problems experienced in many dales houses: poor draught requiring lengthened flues.

This wedding at Outhgill in the early 1920s was that of Lena Metcalfe of Moor Rigg. The family, with father Edgar and mother Rachel, are seen posing after the ceremony.

Pendragon Castle, Mallerstang about 1905, by Thompsons of Kendal in their 'Avenue' series. Surrounded by legend since the Dark Ages, the ruins of the castle are a shadow of the former glory of the place. Restored by Lady Anne Clifford in 1660 after it had been in ruins for over a century, it was again dismantled in 1685 by the Earl of Thanet who had inherited Lady Anne's estates. This castle, with its neighbour, Lammerside Castle, are among the most neglected ancient monuments in Westmorland.

Nateby about 1905, with the Congregational chapel built in 1875 and now the Methodist chapel. Thomas Dixon of Rakehead was Chairman of the Parish Meeting as well as a manager of the school with James Paley of Low Farm, William Alderson of Thrim Gill, Richard Wharton of Low House, Wharton, and James Littlefair of Hartley. Miss Mary Agnes Woof was the schoolmistress. 'The village of Nateby occupies a romantic site,' says a 1905 guide. What would the writer think of the village today?

Wharton Hall dates back to at least the fifteenth century, and was the home of the Wharton family. Sir Thomas Wharton was one of Henry VIII's men and was knighted for thrashing the Scots at Sollom Moss. The fourth Lord Wharton (Philip) was a Parliamentarian colonel under Cromwell, and his son Thomas, the fifth Lord, was active in the 'Revolution' of 1688 which placed William of Orange on the throne. He is reported to have written the jaunty tune 'Lillibullero' for the Protestant armies of King William, a tune which has for many years been broadcast as a 'signature tune', with no sensitivity as to its origins, by the BBC Overseas Service. Thomas was created an earl for his efforts in opposing the Tories in the time of Queen Anne. His son was also a Whig and was created Duke Wharton, but then he changed in every way, becoming first a Tory, then a Catholic Jacobite, and later an officer in the Spanish Army which attacked Gibraltar, before entering a convent in Spain where he died at 32 years of age in 1731, the last of the Whartons and a traitor to all the family causes since the Reformation. Their Hall has long been just a farm, and was occupied by J.T. Dargue when this photograph of about 1905 was taken. (See p. 160.)

High Stenkrith, Kirkby Stephen, photographed by the Photochrom Company of London about 1905. It's a case of find the three boys. The Mannex Guide of 1885 tells its readers that 'the rock is a calcareo-magnesian conglomerate – this can be advantageously studied at Stenkrith Bridge . . . where it forms broad floors stretching across the Eden.'

Merrygill, Hartley, with a solid-wheeled and solid-tyred open tourer car, in a photograph by J.W. Braithwaite and Sons, printers of Kirkby Stephen, in the days before the Second World War when the quarry traffic went by rail.

Castle Lane, Hartley in 1954, with Mrs Jean Marsh and her dog Whiskey. The lane takes its name from Hartley Castle of the Musgrave family, which stood nearby until taken down to repair Eden Hall near Penrith.

We're taking a Flying Visit to KIRKBY STEPHEN.

A holiday postcard from Kirkby Stephen by the national postcard company of Wildt and Kray. This was posted in May 1915 to the Morris Steam Car and Wagon Works at Hunslet near Leeds. The attractions of the area had been opened to holiday-makers by the two railway companies which served the town.

The Merrygill viaduct in 1955, with an Ivatt 2–6–0 No. 46473 returning coal wagons from the north-west (probably Barrow) to the north-east. The train pulls up the 'drag' from Kirkby Stephen towards Stainmore summit.

The Darlington to Penrith evening train calls at Kirkby Stephen East railway station in 1955 with Miss Catherine Marsh awaiting its arrival. This station closed in January 1962.

Kirkby Stephen East railway station and bridge as seen from the nearby park, in a Valentines of Dundee postcard which was used for New Year's greetings in 1908. The neat and slightly imposing Edwardian design of the park and the railway station approach into Kirkby Stephen from the south have been lost today.

The Fountain Café in Kirkby Stephen, run by Mr and Mrs Michael McIlroy was, in the 1950s, a favourite stopping spot for the north-east to Blackpool buses. The last days of the once famous Closes Stores can be seen on the right, and the fish and fruit business of W.J. Haughey is on the left.

The May Queen, as arranged by Mr J.C. Parkinson, on a windy day at Hills Bottoms about 1910, with Miss Rachel Smith, the pupil teacher at the local school acting as the queen. 'When Kirkby Stephen had a may queen and maypole,' says the postcard.

St Luke's Fair at Kirkby Stephen, 27 October 1911. Over the centuries Kirkby Stephen became famous for the market and special fairs which were accommodated in the wide area of the street and Market Place. The October St Luke's Fair filled the town with sheep and gained the name 't' tup fair'. There were many complaints about the mess left in the street by St Luke's Fair animals.

The knife grinder calls in Kirkby Stephen main street in 1954. The time was drawing to a close for the itinerant traders such as this man, who visited the towns and villages on both sides of the northern Pennines.

The Court Room at Kirkby Stephen was behind the police station built in High Street in 1887. It hardly changed over all the years it was used. The door on the left behind the magistrates' bench led to the police station. The small railed enclosure was the witness stand. This view is of about 1905 when Mr Richard Thomas Roe Walton Hallam, Solicitor and Commissioner for Oaths of Hallam and Son, Market Square was the Clerk, and Sergeant Edward Storey occupied the police house part of the building.

The consecration of the 1865 Congregational chapel as a Roman Catholic church of the Holy Family caused some stir at the time, but this little church witnessed even greater controversy, which was reported in the *Cumberland and Westmorland Herald*, when Prince Charles, on holiday in Garsdale, attended the Sunday Catholic mass held here in September 1986. In the background, taking a photograph in 1954, is David Williams MPS, the manager of Boots the Chemists shop, then sited further along the street. The church is now a shop.

The Market Place at the turn of the century, when William Tyson had the Black Bull Hotel, by the Photochrom Company. The shop of A. Bell and Sons, china and glass dealers, can be seen on the right. A train must have been due, as both the Black Bull and the Kings Arms buses are horsed up, ready to go.

The snowstorm of February 1955 completely cut Kirkby Stephen off by rail and road. On 25 February even the Westmorland County Council ex-WD armoured troop carrier with snow plough attached got itself stuck in one of the many drifts and had to be dug out.

The gathering in the Market Square for the Peace Celebration day in 1918 included the schoolchildren and the combined choirs who were conducted by Mr John Stewart, headmaster at the Primary School, who can be seen standing on a table. Two crosses mark a lady, Mrs Norah Ewbank. In the background is the premises of printers and publishers J.W. Braithwaite and Son, and next to the Cloisters is Joseph Bowerbank's, the ironmongers, advertising Kynoch cartridges.

Market Street, Kirkby Stephen at the turn of the century. The view, by Brittain and Wright of Stockton, shows Richard Ivison's watchmakers shop next to the Green Tree Inn when Mary Wilson had the licence. (Is it her cleaning the window?)

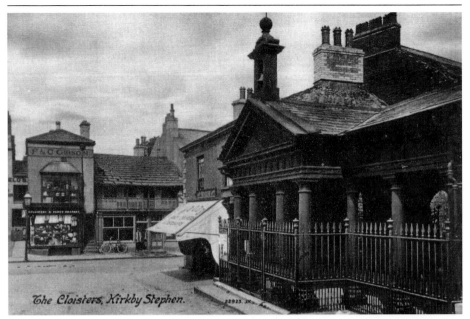

'The Cloisters', Kirkby Stephen are not cloisters at all but the entrance to the churchyard, erected in 1810. In the background of this Valentines of Dundee photograph from the turn of the century is Robert Bousfield's Old Fountain Inn, F.&C. Gibson's Millinery and Fancy Drapery, John Longstaffe's butchers shop in the Shambles and, next to 'the Cloisters', Woods' shop, which has a very fine blind.

Stobars Hall was described in 1897 as 'an elegant mansion, on an elevated site half a mile west of the town, erected in 1829 by the late James Brougham Esq, now the seat of Richard Bovill Thompson, JP.' The Thompsons continued at Stobers until 1940, when the estate went to the Hewetsons, their cousins.

Winton. The first postcard shows the school about 1905, when Miss Mary Elizabeth Jackson was the mistress and the managers were John Reid Sowerby of Winton House, G.E. Thompson, William Dent Morland, John Barker (the postmaster and stocking knitter), and Joseph Lamb from Ewbank House. The second card, from the 1920s, shows an early solid-tyred delivery van and the Baptist chapel. Winton is the birthplace of the eighteenth-century historian Richard Burn who became vicar of Orton and, with Joseph Nicholson, compiled *The History of Cumberland & Westmorland*.

The Belah viaduct was built by Bouch for the North Eastern Railway in July and August 1859. 'Gilkes Wilson with these eighty men raised Belah's Viaduct o'er the Glen.' The statistics – 1,040 ft long, 60 ft span, 196 ft high, 16 iron pillars – were impressive enough for guide books to say this was 'one of the most impressive triumphs of engineering skill in the British Isles'. Triumph or not, the bridge was demolished almost straight after the closure of the line in 1962. Both the photographs are from the very early days and were only reproduced as postcards forty years later.

The North East line after the blizzard on 25 February 1955, when the snowplough engine from Barnard Castle got stuck in a drift near Merrygill, Kirkby Stephen and had to be extracted by men with spades.

The A66 road over Stainmore is on the line of a Roman (and possibly earlier) road. Only the photographer's parked car can be seen in this picture of what is now the busy A66. This moorland area has many ancient monuments to testify its importance in the past and an old reputation for 'nine months winter and three months bad weather'.

High Street, Brough is the title of this Brittain and Wright photograph from the early 1920s. This is where the ascent of Stainmore began, and was to become the scene of many motoring disasters as the A66 became a busy motor road.

Augill Castle, Brough, by J.B. Smithson of Leyburn, about 1905. This is in the parish of Stainmore and was, at the time, the home of a playwright, Paul Kester, who is said to have purchased the estate by cable. The house was built in 1842 by John Bagot Pearson, Pevsner described it as 'A fine essay in early Victorian Castle building.'

George Steadman, facing the camera, wrestles with Hexham Clarke at Grasmere Sports in 1900. The picture, by Mason, is from the end of a long sporting life, as Hexham Clarke was to take the heavyweight title in 1901. Born at Asby on 20 February 1846, George Steadman wrestled from 1865 to 1900, winning the heavyweight title at Grasmere seventeen times. Many of his sixty cups, twenty belts and many medals can now be seen at the Museum of Lakeland Life and Industry at Abbot Hall, Kendal. George died at Brough on Saturday 5 March 1904 and is buried in Brough churchyard.

Brough Hill Fair at the turn of the century in two photographs by E. Metcalfe of Kirkby Stephen. Started by charter in 1331, the Brough Hill Fair, on 30 September and 1 October, developed into a horse fair attended by gypsy and potter folk. Large crowds attended at the beginning of the century and some can be seen in the second picture surrounding a pitch and toss or card game.

Two more views of the Brough Hill Fair. The first, by Valentines, is titled Brough Hill Horse Fair and the second, by Braithwaite and Sons, who had a billposting business in Kirkby Stephen, is from about 1905 and shows a gypsy encampment. Since the plague of 1665 the Brough Hill Fair has been held on land in the nearby parish of Warcop with some participants, from the time of the Second World War, adding the collection of 'scrap' tank gun shell casings to their collection of 'scrap' from surrounding farms.

Hillbeck Hall, Brough about 1905, by Brittain and Wright of Stockton. Hillbeck, or Helbeck, Hall was occupied by the Breeks family at the time. This family had long lived in Warcop and, in the nineteenth century, were much involved with the Indian Civil Service.

First prize winner at Kirkby Stephen in September 1910 was J. Dent of High Ewebank, South Stainmore, seen here with his prize-winning 'Swaddle' (Swaledale) ewe. This is a distinctive breed of sheep off the rough fell sheep commonly seen in Westmorland. The prize for the 'swaddle tup' that year went to J. Dargue of Wharton Hall for his blackfaced Swaledale ram (see p. 160).

King Edward VII's visit to Brougham Hall (see also p. 148), the 'Windsor of the North' and the home of Lord Brougham and Vaux in October 1905. The King had arrived 'indisposed' with a cold, but after a week's stay he was well enough to leave for Raby Castle. The Chief Constable, Mr C. de Courcy Parry travelled by car half an hour before the King's party which was in two cars. These three photographs record the events at Brough as the Chief Constable's car passed through (above) on the way towards Stainmore, and the crowd awaiting the arrival of the King's car. 'There was a great display of flags' records the *Westmorland Gazette* of 2 October 1905. Lord Henry Brougham accompanied by Major General Sir Stanley Clark, the King's Equerry, was in the first car with the King, accompanied by the Honourable Mrs George Keppel following 'in a 40 horse power motor car'. The *Gazette* records that the King passed through Brough at 12.08 p.m.

Brough Castle in the 1930s, photographed by J.L.M. & S.C. in their 'Success' series. Built on the corner of a Roman fort by the Normans, this ancient castle has witnessed the long history of the barony of Westmorland. Destroyed by fire in 1531, rebuilt by Lady Anne Clifford in 1659 and partly demolished by the Earl of Thanet in 1695, only in the 1930s was work started to preserve what was left.

Fox Tower in the parish of Hillbeck was a ruin at the turn of the century. Complete with dining room with fireplace and a spiral stair to the top, the tower is said to have been built to enable the owners of Hillbeck Hall to observe the progress of fox hunts.

Soulby school and church. A 'new' school was erected in 1876, and by 1905, the time of this picture, the school managers were James Park of Laburnum House, Chairman, Toppin Hall, of Low Hall, representing the Parish Meeting, Joseph Rudd of Raw End, Joseph Taylor of Sykeside, William Atkinson of Bridge End, and Thomas Balmer of the Fold. The headteacher was George B. Stanley of Soulby View. John Ashton was the vicar when the picture of the church was taken. St Luke's was built by Sir Philip Musgrave in 1662 and refitted in 1873.

Crosby Garrett's church of St Andrew is said to be have been built on the site of a hill fort. It is an ancient church on an even more ancient holy site of the early Christians. The photograph, by the Photochrom Company of London, dates from the time of the Revd G. Ridley. In the lower picture, taken just after the First World War, can be seen the Midland Railway viaduct, which crossed, to quote an early guide, the 'deep and secluded valley'. The Settle–Carlisle railway put Crosby Garrett in touch with the rest of the country. The railway station was built in a 55 ft deep cutting.

Great Asby children stand in line for this turn of the century picture, blocking the way out of the village. There are three parts to Asby parish: Little Asby, Asby Winderwath and Asby Coatsforth. Great Asby has a fine example of an early Christian Holy Well to Saint Helen, an ancient dedication. The well, like many after Christians lost interest in holy wells, later got a reputation as a healing well. John Gould, George Lamb and William Sawyers lived at North View in those days.

The Club Room at Great Asby, built in 1908, on a picture postcard sent on 10 May 1909 to a Miss Fairer in Caton. 'Dear Maggie, what do you think of this one? I've had some lively times in it, Annie.' Also to be seen is the school. The datestone says 'founded 1688', but it was rebuilt in 1853 and enlarged in 1897.

Cottages in Great Asby on a postcard sent again from Annie to Maggie Fairer, this time at Skipton, 28 August 1908: 'It is our house with Willie Writeson.'

Musgrave Rushbearing takes place on the first Saturday in July, when girls carrying 'crowns' of flowers and boys carrying crosses parade to the church of St Theobald (patron saint of charcoal burners, with a Saint's Day of 1 July). The ceremony probably dates from before Christian times. The photograph is from about 1905 when the Revd Titus Edward Laurie was the vicar. 'After,' says a report of the time, 'the children are regaled with tea, buns etc, presents are distributed amongst them, and the evening is spent in dancing by parents and friends.'

Warcop church of St Columba was under the care of the Abbey at Shap until the Reformation. It is another church where the annual laying of the rush floor continued to be celebrated long after the church floor no longer required it (see p. 106). This picture is by Atkinson and Pollitt of Kendal in the 1920s.

The Rectory at Warcop on a postcard sent to West Wilton Vicarage on 30 September 1910. The Revd Seymour Shaw was the vicar at the time. In recent years the building has been sold off by the Church.

Warcop War Memorial in the 1920s can be seen in the top picture, and Station Road from the same period in the lower view, both photographed by Atkinson and Pollitt of Kendal. The Station Inn took its name from the now closed railway station on the North Eastern Railway from Penrith via Kirkby Stephen and Stainmore into County Durham.

The altar at Warcop church decorated for the 1911 rushbearing.

The procession through the village at about the same time. The pagan midsummer festival was combined in the Christian religion with the midsummer Saint Peter's Day celebration and, amazingly, at churches such as Warcop, and nearby Musgrave, as well as Grasmere and Ambleside, the pre-Christian celebrations, changed to dressing the church, survived the centuries and remain a focal point of the village year. In Warcop the celebrations are on St Peter's Day itself (29 June) while the others are in July.

Warcop Rushbearing participants at Warcop Hall in the 1909 celebrations. Behind the band, the banner of the Reading Society and the St Peter's Day banner ('For old lang syn') can be seen. The school and Reading Society children pose with their wreaths and the flower crowns, with hardly a smile to be seen. Warcop Hall grounds were the centre of events after the service in the church and, 'a tent having been previously erected and decorated with evergreens,' said an 1884 report, 'a monster tea party is held in the afternoon and the remainder of the day is spent in dancing and other innocent amusements.'

High Green Park, Warcop, photographed by Atkinson and Pollitt in the late 1920s.

Sandford in the late 1920s, again by Atkinson and Pollitt, showing the hamlet in Warcop parish where almost all the inhabitants were involved in agriculture, as had been so for many centuries. The roads were unmade even then. Note the heap of stones for filling in potholes.

Sandford about 1910. The Association chapel of 1848 is on the right. Sandford was probably another spot with early Christian connections, as the Hall well and its now lost chapel seem to indicate. The early history of the Warcop and Sandford areas has yet to be written. There are many sites and monuments to attest to its importance.

Ormside railway station on the Midland Railway about 1905 when George Palmer was the station master. Tom Bowman, the signalman, and William Briton, the foreman plate-layer, lived in the nearby cottages. The neatness of the station and its precinct is remarkable.

Ormside Hall about 1905 when Thomas Udale was the farmer. The very ancient settlement of Ormside would appear to have been more important in antiquity than it is today, a reduced village. It is thought that the tower on the right dates to the fourteenth century. Many ancient artefacts found in the area of the church and the hall attest to the truth in legends of ancient importance.

The volunteer camps on Brackenber Moor always included an officers' mess and here, posing very casually, are mess staff in 1913. The horrors of the 'Great War' were only months away.

The rifle range at Hilton backed on to Mell Fell. This was used by the volunteers from nearby Brackenber Moor camp and, during the Second World War, became part of the extensive Warcop gun ranges.

The New Inn at Murton about 1905 when John McHaffie held the licence. Murton, with the adjoining Hilton, had at one time the reputation for the finest water supply in all England. This point of some pride in the parish would not necessarily have impressed Mr McHaffie's clients.

Murton village. This is hardly an industrial scene, but the area surrounding the village has been extensively investigated for lead and other minerals. Had the discoveries proved worth exploiting on a scale larger than the mining that was carried out, there would have been a very different scene than this, photographed by Lillywhite just after the First World War.

Foresters House, Flakebridge about 1905, when occupied by Johnston Tuer, head forester, in the parish of Murton but described as 'near Appleby'. Archibald Bell and Joseph Bowman are shown as foresters. Head sawyer was Thomas Wilkinson and assistant was John E. Bowman.

Bongate Mill, Appleby seen from the castle walls about 1914, showing the ancient strip fields arrangement in the background and the working mill in the foreground. In the Middle Ages, Bongate (or Old Appleby), with its 'parish' church of St Michael, boasted also a Carmelite priory and, nearby, a Premonstratensian leper hospital.

Another general view of Appleby, this time over a cabbage patch with the word 'Appleby' picked out in either cloth or paper on the nearby flower bed. Tom Nelson sent the card to his mother in New Bank Yard, Kendal on 9 August 1907. 'Please have my things and a clean collar,' says the message.

St Anne's Hospital was founded in 1653 by Lady Anne Clifford, with a grant of land in Bongate which had previously been part of the leper hospital estate. 'Mother' and 'Sisters' – thirteen in all – were poor widows of the Borough and received a quarterly pension as well as accommodation. The Valentines postcard was sent on 19 January 1904 to Miss Murray at Kirkby Thore to say, 'We had a great fire at Tufton Arms last night.' (See p. 117.)

Boroughgate from the castle entrance about 1902, by Valentines, showing a deserted unmade street and 'High Cross', one of the two pillars at each end of Boroughgate.

Boroughgate from St Lawrence's church tower, by Sankey of Barrow for Evans of Appleby, about the time of the First World War. Both pillars can be seen, with 'Low Cross' in the foreground. This remarkable street scene, the avenue from the castle to the church, survives more or less intact. Cycles and farmers' carriages are parked where motor cars park today.

St Lawrence's church and 'The Cloisters' about 1910 with a North Eastern Railway delivery cart and advertising for Teasdale and Wright, seedcake and manure merchants (only open Saturdays), and John F. Park's Central Hairdressing Rooms and tobacconist and toy dealer. The church of St Lawrence is said to have been rebuilt in 1176 and is probably as ancient in origin as any in the county. 'The Cloisters' were rebuilt in 1811 by the famous architect of the day Sir Robert Smirke.

The turn out for the Appleby Assizes which was held in the Moot Hall Court Room. In the background is the Whitwell Mark and Co. (of Kendal) Commercial Inn, 'Celebrated ales and stout on draught'.

The Tufton Arms Hotel, with Furnass & Sons' Drapery to the right. The Tufton Arms advertised in 1905: 'John Halifax, family and commercial, posting, free fishing, golf, billiards, motor accommodation, Pit petrol.' At 10 p.m. on Monday 18 January 1904 the Panhard car of a barrister visiting the winter assize caught fire in the coach house and the resulting blaze damaged a wagonette and a hearse.

Bridge Street, Appleby, with Mrs Yare's Temperance Hotel in the background in Bridge House and J.S. Rigg's King's Head Hotel on the right (they advertised as 'the oldest commercial and posting hotel in the Eden Valley – omnibus at the station at the arrival of each train'). W.S. Blake's boot, shoe and cycle shop, Richard Pearson's ironmongers shop, and Sweeton's dressmakers are also to be seen.

Battlebarrow, Appleby about 1902, by J. Whitehead and Sons, stationers and printers of Bridge Street, Appleby. The corset works of James Horn and Son, 'staymakers', is on the left. Everyone stops for the camera.

St Michael's church, Appleby, photographed by Valentines of Dundee, is another church of ancient origin, rebuilt in 'old Appleby' in the fourteenth century and refurbished by Lady Anne Clifford to become, in our own age, a house. The building and the surrounding area have many architectural fragments of earlier churches.

The Wesleyan church on the Sands at Appleby about 1905 at what appears to be harvest festival time. This church was built in 1888 in place of the first church dating from 1823. Many improvements were made in 1904.

Caesar's Tower, Appleby Castle has nothing to do with Caesar but is the tower of a Norman motte and bailey castle which was retained as the castle was improved over the centuries following Norman times. The postcard, posted 26 August 1918, records a visit with the comments 'the old rooms, the staircases and ceilings are falling down in many places.'

Appleby Castle courtyard on a pre-First World War view of this home of the Barons of Westmorland, when it was occupied by Sir Henry James Tufton DL, JP (the Rt. Hon. Lord Hothfield), who owned the castle from 1871 to 1926.

The River Eden in flood at Appleby in a turn of the century view by Whitehead and Sons of Appleby. The Sands shop of John Parkin, grocer and provision dealer (who also had a shop in the Market Hall) and Frederick James Salkeld's Drapery are just above the water line, the dog proving the water on the road is not as deep as might be thought. The rowing boat in the Evans of Appleby view (below) would appear to suggest a greater depth in a 1930s flood.

Appleby New Fair time, in a further turn of the century view by Whitehead of Appleby. The horses are brought down to the Eden at the Sands. Held on the second Tuesday and Wednesday in June, this horse fair has its roots deep in history and, like Brough Hill Fair, was part of the round of the itinerant gypsy and 'potter' folk who 'dealt' in many things other than horses.

The bowling green and tennis courts at Appleby just before the First World War. Tom Bell was the secretary of the Appleby Bowling and Lawn Tennis Association at the time.

This charming study of, presumably, father and daughter from the 1880s is an example of a carte-de-visite photograph from the studio of J. Huff and Son, early photographers at Penrith and Appleby.

Two pictures of the Band of Hope Demonstration at Appleby on 16 June 1910. The top photograph is from the 'Romney Studio', photographers of Carlisle. The card was posted to Mrs Ewbank of 14 Victoria Square, Kirkby Stephen on 24 June 1916 by Lizzie Hebson of Appleby. Members of all the local Westmorland community Bands of Hope attended with their banners. The event was supported by many clergy and the school teachers. A strong demonstration for God and against drink. The lower picture shows the banners from Brough and Hoff among others.

Bewley Castle, 'near Colby' is in fact in the parish of Bolton. The castle dates from the twelfth or thirteenth centuries and was for a long time the property of the Bishops of Carlisle. This 'Dalton' series postcard shows a part of the ruin at a time when William Edmondson was the tenant at Old Bewley Farm nearby and Robert Burra was the landowner.

South View, Colby in a photograph obviously intended for the family to use as a greeting card. The card was sent by 'Billy' to his mother. 'Will you please get us a loaf of bread and some milk for Monday.' Many will agree that times have not changed in this respect. Was 'Billy' the William Haigh who lived at South View in the 1920s?

Netherhoff, Colby just after the First World War. 'This is one of the most picturesque places in this district and the house of one of Fred's uncles,' says the message from J. Molyneux on the back of the postcard. Fred's uncle would be Mr Thomas Wills who was at Netherhoff at the time.

Crackenthorpe Hall, on a postcard sent on 22 December 1905 when Joseph Torbock JP lived there. 'Best wishes for Christmas and New Year' to Miss Rawlinson of St Albans, 'from F.H.T.' Joseph Torbock was tenant of the Machell family at the time and his wife was Florence Hoste Torbock (neé Henley). Crackenthorpe was home to the Machell family from very early times. Thomas Machell (1647–98) wrote a history of Westmorland full of carefully noted facts in an indecipherable hand writing which is therefore still awaiting full publication.

Bolton church, on a postcard sent in July 1911, another of Westmorland's ancient churches with much twelfth-century stonework still to be seen. The message – 'This church is 800 years old' – on the back may well be an underestimate of the true age.

Bolton village, on a postcard posted to Darlington at Christmas 1912. Until 1753 the curate at Bolton lived on 'the produce of the chapelyard, and the tithes of the garths, chickens, eggs, ducks, hemp and flax in the Lordship of Bolton'.

Dent's Cottage, Bolton about 1910. The Dent family of Flass, Maulds Meaburn were major landowners in Bolton parish. Robert W. Dent of Flass was the County Councillor, Joseph Crosby Dent of Prospect House was Rural District Councillor and school manager, and John Henry Dent of Elm House was Clerk to the Parish Council.

The Masons Arms, Long Marton, Appleby about 1905 when Sarah Strong had the licence. The Parish Council at the time consisted of John Dobson, the Clerk, Edmund Thompson JP of Manor House, the Chairman, and members James Raper Highmoor of Ivy House, Isaac Dodd of Broad Lea, Brampton, Robert Butterworth of Croft End, Brampton, William Hull of Knock Hall, John Watson of Knock End, Thomas Johnstone of Mid Town Farm and Christopher Simpson of Long Marton. Edmund Thompson was also County Councillor, Rural District Councillor, school manager and Hon. Secretary of the Parish Institute.

'An Old World Bridge' is the title of this Beatys of Carlisle view of Long Marton in the 1930s. Although the village and its church are of ancient origin, the nineteenth century saw the place 'modernized'. In 1880 the church was given a 'thorough restoration' and 'the internal fittings replaced with others of a more elaborate design'.

The huge Midland Railway embankment, railway cottages and the railway station in the background make this an odd view of Long Marton about 1910. The picture is by Broughton of Burnley. The station closed in 1968.

The Institute at Long Marton in a 1920s photograph by Beatys of Carlisle. Conceived and financed by the Revd Hay Macdowall Erskine, then vicar at St Margaret and St James' church, the Institute was built in 1893 at a cost of £750 to provide a reading room (with newspapers), a library, and a meeting room on the first floor.

Laurel Bank, Long Marton in another 1910 view by Broughton of Burnley. Miss Annie Moorcroft lived there at the time and advertised 'apartments'.

Dufton Green about 1910. 'Little has changed here since the days of our great grand-fathers' says an 1885 guide. The fountain on the green was erected by the London Lead Company in 1858 as part of a new water supply following a typhoid epidemic in nearby Teesdale.

Dufton Gill, on a postcard by J. Whitehead and Son of Appleby about 1910. 'What about Jesmond Dene?' says the message on the back.

Knock in about 1910, with unmade roads and a heap of stones for the parish to use to fill in potholes as they appeared. The population was reported to be 97 people living in 907 acres. The village had a postal wall letterbox that was 'cleared at 4 p.m. on weekdays only'.

Knock Village and Dufton Pike, by J. Whitehead of Appleby about 1910. The village shoemaker was William Robson, and John Lightburn had the village shop. Joseph Liddle had the licence of the Packhorse public house.

Kirkby Thore at about the time of the First World War. The village has never recovered the importance it enjoyed in Roman times.

The Kirkby Thore Band of Hope with their banner in the road in the 1920s. A very serious group of youngsters. At this time the *Herald* newspaper carried many reports of difficulties inside the Temperance movement and arguments for and against their activities.

The bridge at Kirkby Thore on a postcard sent on 17 October 1910 to Miss Alderson of the Vicarage, Cliburn. James Ellwood was the carrier to Penrith, assistant overseer and Clerk to the Parish Council. Mrs Agnes Ellwood ran an alabaster manufacturing business. The Misses Ellwood were dressmakers, grocers and drapers, and Tom Ellwood was the blacksmith.

The Kings Arms at Temple Sowerby is an old coaching inn on the main Carlisle to Yorkshire road. The view is from about 1910, when John Furness ran the hotel as well as being a 'farmer'. Note the terrible state of the unmade road (see p. 136).

The unmade main road through Temple Sowerby. The maypole is on the right and the Kings Arms is in the distance. It was quite safe then for children to play and hens to roam. John William Sisson of Vicarage House, Thomas Goulding of West View, James C. Lancaster of Skygarth, Joseph Kitchen of Linden House and Joseph Sisson the blacksmith were on the Parish Council which discussed the road problems.

The Green at Temple Sowerby about 1910 showing junior cricket practice on what was obviously a well used pitch. Miss Rebecca Nicholson advertised as dressmaker, and Robert and John Nicholson as joiners, cartwrights and builders (fitters up of marquees, etc). Their services would have been in demand following restoration of the May Queen Festival from 1908.

Kate Pearson was the Temple Sowerby Rose Queen on 2 June 1910 when, as the *Mid Cumberland and North Westmorland Herald* records, 'the pretty spectacle was marred by rain'. 'The fete takes the form of a costume procession, maypole and Morris dances, and a programme of sports, finishing with a dance in the evening' said the *Herald*. The parade formed near the village green at about two o'clock, headed by two marshals, Dr Stevenson and Mr Hastings dressed as deputy lieutenants, who led the Culgaith Brass Band, a detachment of the Cumberland and Westmorland Yeomanry and a number of boy scouts. Two boys, Richard Goulding and John Halmshaw, travelled on the queen's carriage and the queen's attendants were Minnie, Lizzie and Rachel Bird, Annie and Lizzie Armstrong, Nellie Leggett, Isobel Hodgson and Elsie Robinson. Numerous decorated carts and cycles and dancing groups were also included.

'The Fairy Queen Court' at the Thursday 14 May 1908 May Queen Festival was declared the most effective tableau by the *Herald* newspaper. The Fairy Queen was Miss Hilda Hanson, who was surrounded by a number of girls 'almost lost in a mass of primroses'. The May Queen that year was the vicar's daughter Ethel Anderson.

The May Queen Festival of 2 June 1910, again showing Kate Pearson, but this time on her 'perfect floral bower', to quote the *Herald*, with a dapple grey horse. 'She made a very pretty picture in her white robe and veil with a chaplet of roses on her head.' The crown bearer was Master W. Cleasby, the sceptre bearer Master Tom Sisson and the garland bearer Master Tom Clark.

The 1908 May Day festivities at the maypole with the two marshals, Dr Stevenson and Mr Hastings, dressed as Yeomen of the Guard, arranging the court around May Queen Ethel Anderson, the daughter of the vicar, before Dr Stevenson read the proclamation and the queen was crowned with a 'chaplet of flowers' and presented with a garland and a sceptre of flowers. This was the first May Day festivity after a lapse of twenty-four years and coincided with a gift to the village of a 75 ft maypole by Lord Hothfield of Appleby.

St. James's church, Temple Sowerby about 1910, when 'Thomas Watson Anderson MA (Queens College, Oxford)' was shown as vicar. Note the large heap of hay awaiting collection from the graveyard. St James's church appears to date from the fourteenth century but was completely rebuilt in 1770 and 1877. 'The 1770 tower is now the oldest part of the church,' said a guide of the times.

Hill View, Temple Sowerby about 1905 when Mrs Hannah Jackson and Mrs Margaret Atkinson are listed as occupiers. Temple Sowerby railway station, 'Eden valley branch of the North Eastern Railway', had William Appleby as station master at the time. The County Councillor was George Lowis of Ash Hill, and John William Sisson, auctioneer of Vicarage House, was Parish Council chairman and District Councillor.

A pretty cottage, Temple Sowerby is the title of this view of Sycamore Cottage about 1905. Miss Murray of Elm Lodge, Ravenstonedale is asked on the postcard, 'Please send the recipe for vegetable marrow jam as we are going to make some. This is Mr R's house – the man with the black dog sent to you before.' Worthy of note is the rather elaborate extension of the bedroom window box and the sliding window.

Acorn Bank, Temple Sowerby, again about 1905, was occupied by the recently widowed Mrs Hannah Boazman who had lost her husband Henry in 1904, leaving her as the Lady of the Manor of Temple Sowerby.

The Scaur, Temple Sowerby was another rural 'visitors view' to help postcard sales. This photograph of about 1910 is by J. Whitehead and Sons of Appleby.

Eden Bridge, on the road from Temple Sowerby to Penrith, was a hive of activity when Reeds of Penrith took their picture about 1905. Children play in the foreground and workmen with ladders can be seen on the bridge. The River Eden runs into the county of Cumberland near here.

Whinfell House about 1905 when Richard Burne was the farmer. He was also a manager of the local school. An ancient deer park for Brougham Castle, with a common enclosed in the eighteenth century and 900 acres planted as woodland, Whinfell is a part of the ancient parish of Brougham.

On the green at Milburn on the border with Cumberland. This is another of J. Whitehead of Appleby's pictures from before the First World War. The maypole and the school and lots of children and a flock of geese under the chestnut tree can be seen. The maypole is said to be on a Celtic burial site and the village green itself has been used by the parish for centuries in activities that probably date from that period.

On the A66 road at the Countess's Pillar in the 1920s, by Atkinson and Pollitt of Kendal. The motor bus is the only traffic to be seen. The road here crosses a Roman cemetery which was discovered when improvements were carried out in recent decades. Lady Anne Clifford had the pillar erected in 1656 on the spot where she last saw her mother, Lady Margaret, on 2 April 1616.

Brougham Castle guarding the ancient crossing point of the River Eamont, the boundary at one time between Scotland and England and later Cumberland and Westmorland. The photograph is by the national photographic company, Stengal of London. The castle was built in the corner of a Roman fort, as at Brough, by the Normans and was much expanded in the medieval period. The home of the Clifford family for many centuries, this is where Lady Anne died in 1675. The castle then fell into ruin.

SECTION THREE

The River Eamont
to Ullswater

Brougham Hall about 1902, by Friths of Reigate. This shows the 'Windsor of the North' from the garden side when Lord Henry Brougham was the occupier.

The view from the bridge which connected the Hall to its nearby church, by Reeds of Penrith. After the death of Lord Henry Brougham, the 4th Lord Victor Henry Peter Brougham, who, it is said, became famous in song for breaking the bank at Monte Carlo (he did it twice), ended up losing so much in gambling that he had to sell the Hall and its contents. The Brougham family had not been popular in the past with the local Tory landowners; the Broughams had a history of Liberalism going back generations. That unpopularity was apparently manifested when Geoffrey Carleton Cooper, of Carleton Hall across the River Eamont in Cumberland, in a notable act of vandalism which the County Council were only able to curtail when most of the damage had been done, bought the Hall and set about its demolition in 1934.

Brougham Hall from the courtyard, in the Wrench and Co. 'Reliable' series from about 1910.

The Brougham chapel, next to Brougham Hall, by Stengal and Company. The words 'this is close to where the King is staying', have been added, a reference to the visit of King Edward VII in October 1905 (see pp. 96 and 97). The chapel to St Wilfred was rebuilt by Lady Anne Clifford in 1658 and was 'improved and beautified' internally by many generations of the Brougham family.

A servant's view of the King in a carriage at Brougham Hall on the October 1905 visit to Lord Henry Brougham. The constitutional crisis of 1909, when the Tory Lords rejected the 'peoples' budget' of the Liberal Commons, was in the making. There is no doubt that whilst at Brougham the King would have talked over matters with Lord Henry Brougham following the Liberal revival of 1905. Free secondary education was introduced in 1902, Childrens Acts were being planned, as were the Old Age Pension (of 1908) and Labour Exchanges (1909). The King, like William IV before him, is said to have taken a great interest in these matters but was to die (in 1910) in the middle of the crisis over the cost of their introduction. The circumstances were reminiscent of the period when the 1832 Reform Act was being carried through by Lord Chancellor Henry Peter Brougham, which resulted in the landowning classes sharing government with the 'middle classes' on a property qualification franchise and helped avert revolution in Britain.

Eamont Bridge, with the 'Welcome to Cumberland' sign which greeted northbound travellers for many years. The photograph of about 1905 is by Brittain and Wright in their 'Phoenix' series. All that can be seen was in the county of Cumberland.

Eamont Bridge by Reeds of Penrith about 1905. Mr G. Reed of Penrith took many photographs of places and events in the area and sold the pictures as postcards. The ancient bridging point of this one time boundary of England and Scotland was a favourite venue for walks from Penrith until the motor car changed the surrounding area for ever.

The Westmorland and Cumberland Yeomanry passing through Eamont Bridge on their way to a camping ground in Lowther Park. This is one of a series published by Reeds of Penrith about 1905. The local volunteers are seen on their way to the annual camp in the park of their colonel to train for the horrors of the First World War, the Boer War having just finished.

Eamont Bridge village in the 1920s, by Atkinson and Pollitt of Kendal, with little traffic on the A6 road leading to the bridge over the Eamont. Traffic chaos was to follow in the next decades as the A6 road crossed the narrow bridge at this point.

Yanwath Hall, by Reeds of Penrith, about 1905 when Thomas Bird was the farmer. Yanwath Hall dates from medieval times but had been a farm on the Lowther estate for many years. Besides farming, Thomas Bird was County Councillor, Rural District Councillor, Chairman of the Parish Meeting and chairman of the school managers.

The entrance to Lowther Park at Eamont Bridge in a photograph by Stengal and Company about 1902. There are a number of henge monuments in this area of north Westmorland which testify to the great age and importance of the settlements hereabouts and it seems unfortunate that one was lost to make way for this entrance gate.

Lowther Castle was rebuilt by the architect Sir Robert Smirke in 1806–11, and is seen in this picture by Reeds of Penrith in the days of the 'Yellow Earl', Hugh Lowther the 5th Earl of Lonsdale, who was the last of the Lowthers to occupy the castle. The earl gave his colours to the Automobile Association (he was its first President) and the local Tory Party whom, it is said, he told to adopt his colours or do without his support. During the Second World War the estate was taken over by the army, and after the war and Hugh Lowther's death in 1944 the contents of the castle were sold in a most amazing 'bargain sale', which is still talked of today. The castle was then gutted and reduced to a shell.

In the second picture by D. Knights-Whittome of Sutton, Surrey from about 1905, the entrance hall can be seen with trophies and paintings on display.

Red deer in Lowther Park about 1905. The park was said to be 2,300 acres in extent. Donald Stewart of Park House, Lowther was the deerkeeper in those days, and Frederick Clarke of Lowther New Town head gardener – they must have argued often! William Jones of South View and Charles Robinson of Lowther village were listed as gamekeepers.

Hugh Cecil Lowther with his wife Lady Grace Cicelie attending, as they frequently did, an event in the district about 1902. The photograph is by Fearnside of Penrith. Lady Grace was the third daughter of the Marquis of Huntly. Lord Lonsdale's local titles included Deputy Lieutenant for Cumberland and Westmorland, Colonel of the Westmorland and Cumberland Imperial Yeomanry, and Honorary Colonel of the 3rd Battalion of the Border Regiment and of the Cumberland Artillery Volunteers.

Askham village, by Brittain and Wright in their 'Phoenix' series of about 1902, shows the horse trough and the joiners shop behind. James Henry Bateman was joiner, wheelwright, carpenter, hayrake manufacturer and postmaster. Letters arrived by cart from Penrith at 7 a.m. and were despatched at 4.45 p.m.

St Peter's church at Askham was rebuilt by Sir Robert Smirke for Lord Lonsdale on an ancient site by the River Lowther in 1832. This Brittain and Wright photograph shows the church when the Revd Thomas Beaufort Tylecote BA was rector of Lowther and lived opposite in Askham Hall. The Revd John Alfred Kitchin was vicar of Askham and lived in the Vicarage.

Thomas Moss's grocers shop in Askham about 1905, by Reeds of Penrith. Thomas was also a manager of the school with the Revds Mr Kitchin and Mr Tylecote, William Bowman of Askham Gate, William Clark of Widewath and Robert Cooper of Keld Head.

The bridge over the River Lowther at Askham about 1902, on a photograph sold by Reeds of Penrith as a coloured postcard. The Lowther, flowing down to the Eamont and the Eden past Shap Abbey and Lowther Castle, through some of the most historical and beautiful countryside in the land, is worthily depicted here.

The view from Askham across Lowther Park and into the valley of the Eden in the 1930s, by Atkinson and Pollitt of Kendal. Almost all that can be seen was Lowther land.

The Friends Meeting House at Tirril in this early (possibly late nineteenth-century) post-card view by Reeds of Penrith. The Meeting House, built in 1733, had been converted into a reading room by this time. The grounds contain the grave of Kendal man Charles Gough who died on Helvellyn in 1805 and was guarded by his dog for three months. Both William Wordsworth, whose father lived near here, and Sir Walter Scott used the story of canine fidelity in their works.

Pooley Bridge from Dunmallet ancient hill fort in the 1930s, by Atkinson and Pollitt of Kendal. This is the ancient crossing point of the Eamont as it leaves Ullswater on its way to join the Eden.

The Crown Hotel, Pooley Bridge, by S.M. Gibson and Company of Gateshead, when T.H. Yeates was the proprietor. Rooms could be had for 2s., breakfast and tea were from 1s. 6d. and dinner from 2s. 6d. Pension was 7s. a day or 42s. a week.

The Pooley Bridge pier on Ullswater is in the county of Cumberland. The steam boat *Raven* is at the pier. The waters of Ullswater go out to sea down the River Eden via the Eamont.

Dunmallet and Ullswater from the Westmorland side about 1902 by the Pictorial Stationery Company in their 'Peacock' series. Dunmallet is topped by an ancient hill fort guarding the crossing below.

Howtown Hotel on a postcard of 1904, which was posted in July 1905 saying, 'This is the picture taken by Mr Baldry last year.' The Howtown Hotel was then occupied by Walter Baldry who advertised 'Posting and Pleasure Boats'. Walter was also a school manager.

The *Raven* in Howtown Bay, Ullswater about 1905 by Reeds of Penrith brings the book to a close. For the rest of Ullswater in Westmorland see *The Westmorland Lakes in Old Photographs*.

J. Dargue of Wharton Hall with his prizewinning Swaledale ram (or Swaddle Tup) which took first prize at Kirkby Stephen in September 1910. A prize-winning sheep, from a land of sheep, from the home of the Lords Wharton who at one time had so much power in the Eden Valley.

Acknowledgements

The production of this book would not have been possible without the assistance, in various ways, of the following: Mrs Jean Marsh; Victoria Slowe and Janet Dugdale of Abbot Hall, who encouraged the start of the project; Christine Strickland and Sylvia Mallinson of the Kendal Library Local Studies Collection; Mrs E. Baker (née Woof), late of Kendal; Mrs Beattie of Kendal for the George Steadman picture; Mr George Dawson for use of the N. Carradice photographic collection; Mr J. Fairer of Shap; Mr N. Honeyman of Barrow-in-Furness; Mr N. Humphries of Kendal; Mrs L. Knowles (née Huck) of Selside; Mr and Mrs F. Nevinson of Langdale, Selside and Kendal; the editor of the *Westmorland Gazette*; and those people of the area into whose families this book intrudes, and the many others who encourage and support me in the collection of local old photographic images.